A book
is a present you can open
again and again.

THIS BOOK BELONGS TO

FROM

WONDER WHY

All About Pets
with Inspector McQ

Written by Kathleen Kain
Illustrated by Yoshi Miyake

TREASURE TREE™

World Book, Inc.
a Scott Fetzer company
Chicago London Sydney Toronto

Copyright © 1992
World Book, Inc.
525 West Monroe Street
Chicago, Illinois 60661

Printed in the United States of America
ISBN 0-7166-1625-4
Library of Congress Catalog Card No. 91-65744

8 9 10 11 12 13 14 15 99 98 97 96

Cover design by Rosa Cabrera
Book design by Ann Tomasic
Inspector McQ illustrated by Eileen Mueller Neill
Photo, page 5, © Ralph A. Reinhold, Animals Animals
Photo, page 10, © Joyce Wilson, Animals Animals
Photo, pages 20-21, © Hans Reinhold, OKAPIA from
    Photo Researchers
Photo, pages 28-29, © Richard Kolar, Photo Researchers

Hello. My name is Inspector McQuestion, but you can call me McQ. You're tracking down the answers to questions on pets, are you? Well, I'll be very pleased to help. I have a special interest in animals, you know. Ready? Let's see what we can find out.

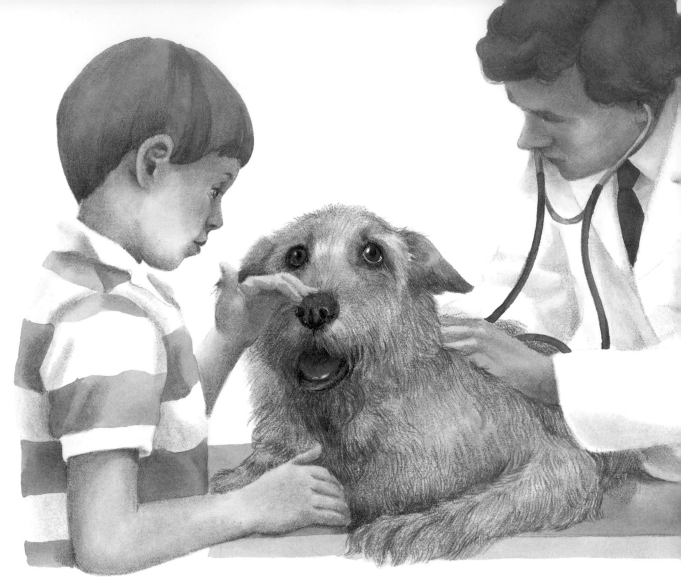

Why is a dog's nose wet ?

Even a truly brilliant detective does not always know the answer. However, this inspector does know who to ask for more information. I checked with a veterinarian to find out about dog noses.

A healthy dog's nose feels cool and wet. That's because the dog's nose discharges a clear, thin liquid. This liquid makes the nose moist. Dogs lick their noses, too, and this helps to keep their noses moist as well. A moist nose keeps a dog's sense of smell keen.

A dog with a hot, dry nose is probably running a fever. Normally, a dog's temperature stays between 101 °F and 102.5 °F (38.3 °C and 39.2 °C). Take your dog to a veterinarian if the dog's nose feels hot and dry.

And remember, too, although all healthy dogs have wet noses, not all dogs with wet noses are healthy. A dog may have a wet nose and still be sick. Other signs of illness in a dog are dull eyes and dry, dull fur.

Do keep in touch with your dog's doctor for any questions about your pet's health. I'm sure you'll find the answers "right on the nose."

Why do dogs pant?

Intriguing question! Let's examine our clues.

Clue Number One

Rex here pants a great deal in hot weather. His tongue hangs out, and he breathes rapidly. Meanwhile, water evaporates from his tongue and throat. (When water evaporates, it turns into a gas. We cannot see the gas, but we can see that a wet surface has dried.)

Clue Number Two

When evaporation takes place on human skin it serves a useful purpose. When people sweat, the water in the sweat evaporates. Water turns very cold as it evaporates. So sweating is the human body's way of cooling off.

Clue Number Three

Do dogs sweat, too? Let's examine Rex and find out. Hmm, it appears that only the pads of his paws sweat very much.

Thus, the answer is simple: Dogs cannot sweat enough to keep their temperature at a normal 101 °F (38.3 °C) in hot weather or during vigorous exercise. So they pant to cool off.

Why are dogs called "man's best friend"?

People really do love their pets! Sometimes they even call dogs their best friends. Have you ever wondered why? Dogs and people go back a long way together. The earliest pet known to scientists was a dog that belonged to a cave dweller. The dog probably helped its owner in hunting for food and by warning of approaching strangers.

Today's dogs help people, too. Some dogs are crime fighters. Take Brandy, for example. Brandy belonged to the bomb squad of the

New York Police Department. One day Brandy and the
police officers she worked with rushed to the airport.
Someone had threatened to bomb a jetliner. After a one-
minute search, Brandy led the officers to a bomb in the
cockpit where the crew sat. Brandy proved to be one of the
best friends that crew ever had!

Dogs have rescued people from fires and led search
teams to people lost in the snow or in the woods. And
they help in everyday ways, too. Dogs keep people
company. Seeing-eye dogs guide the blind. Hearing-ear
dogs alert their deaf owners to doorbells, telephone calls,
smoke alarms, and the like. The list goes on, and the dogs
keep on working. True friends indeed!

Why do cats lick themselves

Now the adventures really begin! I have to be very careful around cats, you understand. But cats are such wonderful pets—for people. Let's get on with it, shall we?

Cats wash themselves with their tongues. Some scientists believe that the saliva, or liquid, in the cat's mouth, cleans like a soap. Have you ever watched a cat carefully lick himself all over? A cat's tongue can reach every part of his body except one—his head. But even a cat's head gets washed. Here's how: The cat licks his foreleg and then rubs the foreleg on his face.

Cats also lick themselves to cool off. When you're hot, you sweat all over and then cool off as the sweat dries. When a cat is hot, only his paw pads sweat. The cat's tongue wets the rest of his body. Then he cools off as the saliva dries.

Now how's this for an opportunity: Tiger here is sleeping, but he will take a great big yawn from time to time. If we look quietly (and very carefully!) we can see the tiny "bristles" on the surface of Tiger's tongue. When the cat licks himself, these tongue bristles brush out dirt and loose fur. The rough tongue also causes the cat's skin to produce oil. This oil waterproofs the cat's fur. The sun turns some of the oil into vitamin D. When Tiger licks his fur again, he will swallow this vitamin so important for strong bones.

Thank you, Tiger, and good-by. I wouldn't want you to wake up and find me here!

How do cats leap from high places safely?

Ready, set, go—off the shelf, into the air, and onto the floor on all fours! How do cats do it?

Watch Lila and how she looks before she leaps. Like people, but unlike mice and dogs, Lila and other cats have eyes in the front of their face. This helps them judge distances fairly well. As a result, cats generally avoid leaping from places that look too high off the ground.

But when Lila does leap, she has several advantages over you and me.

First, Lila's "righting reflex" takes over as soon as her paws hit the air. This natural reaction turns her upright so that she will land on all four feet. Lila uses her eyes and her righting reflex to help keep her balance so her body stays upright throughout the leap.

Second, Lila, as well as most other cats, has a very bendable backbone. When she hits the ground, her back arches into an almost perfect half circle. This cushions the cat's landing and helps prevent broken bones.

Bravo, Lila! Well done.

Why do cats purr ?

Cats purr from purrrre delight. Not a bad joke, if I do say so myself. But now let's take a serious look at purring.

Experts disagree about what makes cats purr. Some say that blood rushing through the blood vessels in a cat's chest makes the purring sound. Blood vessels are the tubes—such as arteries and veins—that carry blood through the body. Others say that purring comes from a cat's throat. This is their explanation:

Behind the "true" vocal cords in a cat's throat are folds called the "false" vocal cords. A cat uses both sets of vocal cords to purr nonstop. When a cat breathes out, the true vocal cords purr softly. When a cat breathes in, the false vocal cords purr more loudly. This is because the incoming air vibrates the folds of the false vocal cords like a bow vibrating the strings on a violin.

Cats use their true vocal cords to do all the rest of their "talking." They have a wide vocabulary, too. Many cat watchers think that cats use about a hundred sounds and tones. Perhaps so. . . but *I* will never stay around a nonsleeping cat long enough to find out!

How do dogs and cats use their tails ?

Dogs and cats use their tails very differently. I ought to know—having spent most of my life observing these awesome creatures from a safe distance!

Take Taffy, here. Her tail is wagging madly. Why? She's so happy her owner is home. Now she has someone to play with. "Ah. . . time for dinner, time for a walk," she's probably thinking, too. (Dogs have such simple pleasures!) The point is, though, dogs wag their tails when they're happy.

Oh, oh, look at Taffy now. Maybe something frightened her. See how her tail is tucked under her back legs? Dogs also tuck in their tails when they're in pain. And they may hold their tails straight up if they're angry at another dog.

As for cats, let's quietly trail Tabby here and see what we can find out.

While her young mistress dresses for school, Tabby purrs and holds her tail straight up as if to say "Good morning!" A little later, she curves her tail into a question mark, and arches her back. I think she's asking for breakfast.

When the mistress leaves for school, Tabby's tail droops. It appears to say, "I'm miserable without company!" Soon the cat spots a ball of yarn. Her tail curves up and over her back as she plays with the ball.

I wonder how Tabby's tail would react to me. I take a deep breath and dash into full view. She sees me and crouches. The tip of the tail quivers. The cat is preparing to pounce.

I'm getting out of here! Looking back, I see she's angry over my quick exit. She fluffs her tail to twice its size and swishes it back and forth. But I don't wait around to find out what Tabby's tail will do next.

Why do dogs and cats sniff at things ?

Dogs and cats use their sense of smell in much the same way. They sniff trees and other objects to find out if friends or strangers are in the neighborhood. What they smell are the scents that dogs and cats (mostly males) spray around their "territory." When dogs or cats recognize their own scent, they know home is near.

Some dogs have especially keen noses. Bloodhounds can follow even a faint scent for miles. They can help find lost people, and they can help police officers sniff out clues to a crime.

Cats seldom use their nose when they hunt, but they do use it when they eat. A cat often refuses food it cannot smell. For instance, a cat with a cold probably will turn up her stuffy nose at a mild-smelling food like chicken. A wise pet owner offers a stuffy-nosed cat strong-smelling tuna instead.

Tuna, indeed! Maybe I should try it sometime.

Are goldfish really gold?

In the case of goldfish, all that glitters is not gold. Examine the evidence for yourself.

Exhibit A

The scales that cover a goldfish have no color. You can see right through them to the fish's skin.

Exhibit B

The skin may or may not be gold-colored. Goldfish skin comes in many other colors: blue, silver, yellow, or orange-red, for example. Or, goldfish may be multi-colored, like the ones you see here in the photograph. Light bounces off their glittery skin, making the fish shine like pieces of jewelry.

No matter what color they are, don't you think goldfish make pretty pets? Goldfish owners can enjoy their pets longer by following a few simple rules:

1. Handle your goldfish carefully. Rough handling can rub off the layer of slime that protects the fish's scales from germs.

2. Feed your fish sparingly. Goldfish eat very little, especially in cold water.

3. Make sure the fish tank is large enough. Goldfish get the oxygen they need to stay alive from the water they swim in. So give them enough water and change it often.

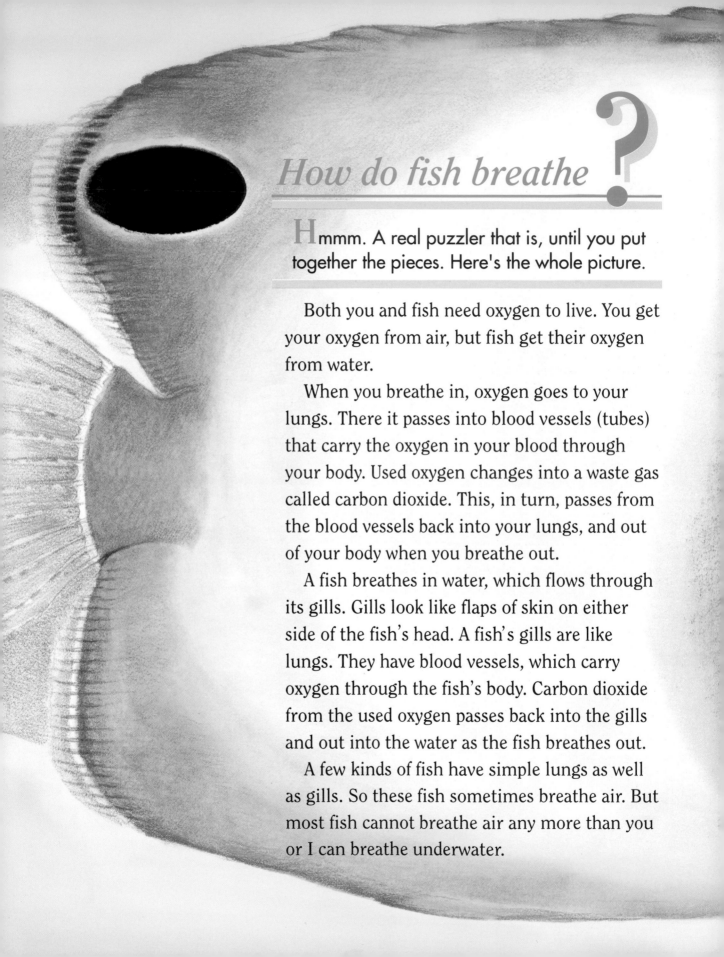

How do fish breathe?

Hmmm. A real puzzler that is, until you put together the pieces. Here's the whole picture.

Both you and fish need oxygen to live. You get your oxygen from air, but fish get their oxygen from water.

When you breathe in, oxygen goes to your lungs. There it passes into blood vessels (tubes) that carry the oxygen in your blood through your body. Used oxygen changes into a waste gas called carbon dioxide. This, in turn, passes from the blood vessels back into your lungs, and out of your body when you breathe out.

A fish breathes in water, which flows through its gills. Gills look like flaps of skin on either side of the fish's head. A fish's gills are like lungs. They have blood vessels, which carry oxygen through the fish's body. Carbon dioxide from the used oxygen passes back into the gills and out into the water as the fish breathes out.

A few kinds of fish have simple lungs as well as gills. So these fish sometimes breathe air. But most fish cannot breathe air any more than you or I can breathe underwater.

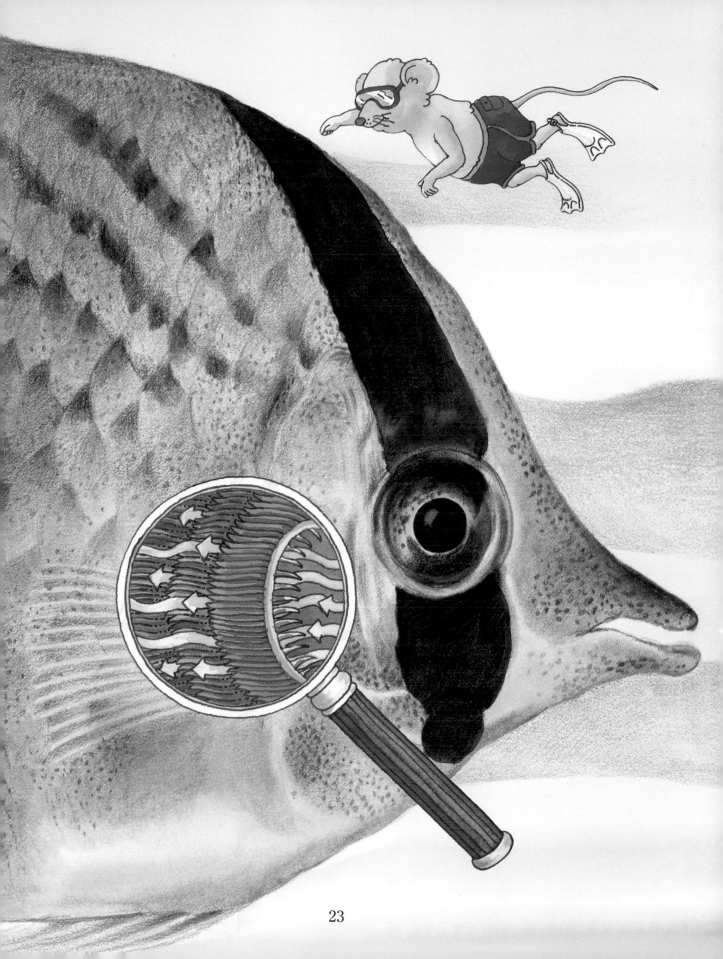

Why do hamsters run around exercise wheels ?

Hamsters happen to be cousins of mine. So I know that they not only run, but also climb, push, and roll. Hamsters love to exercise and they need to.

A hamster should get some kind of exercise, at least for short periods, each day. Otherwise, its muscles may atrophy (AT ruh fee). This means that they lose the power to move.

For a hamster to stay healthy, it should have plenty of room. If you have a hamster, put some action toys in the cage. A hamster can even roll around outside its cage in a see-through plastic ball!

Here are some other tips for a healthy hamster:

1. Feed your hamster treats like lettuce and carrots only once in a while. Hamster food is best for most of the time.

2. Place the cage away from drafts.

3. Hamsters like to sleep during the day. Play with your pet mostly in the early morning or evening.

I admire my cousins' energy and wish someone would give me such nice toys to play with!

How do parrots "talk"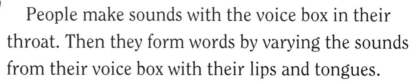?

I've wondered about the same thing myself. So I trailed some bird watchers and listened carefully to their conversations. Here's what I found out.

People make sounds with the voice box in their throat. Then they form words by varying the sounds from their voice box with their lips and tongues.

A syrinx is a bird's version of a person's voice box. Like most birds, parrots make sounds with their syrinx. However, parrots have no lips and barely move their tongue when "talking." So bird watchers think parrots use only their syrinx to make words.

Parrots often connect some words with certain people or times of the day. For example, they may say "good night" in the evening. But they also say words at the wrong time, such as "hello" when their owner leaves the room. So bird watchers have concluded that parrots don't understand what they say.

Parrots seem to whistle even more than they talk. But, again, bird watchers have news for us. Few parrots actually whistle. Most let out a scream that only sounds like a whistle.

I've met some wonderful parrots in my day, and they've helped me with cases. But with all that screaming and chattering, I doubt they would make good detectives. Because, in my line of work, sometimes you need to be as quiet as a mouse.

Are guinea pigs really pigs

Just as I suspected. This science book tells us that guinea pigs are not really pigs. They belong to the rodent family along with yours truly, other mice, and rabbits. And scientists call them cavies. So why does everyone else call them guinea pigs? Here are my ideas.

Ahh, here's something in a book on South America. That's where cavies first came from. The book tells us that South American Indians sold the mouselike creatures for food in their marketplaces. When the early Spanish settlers saw the cavies being prepared for sale, it

reminded them of how they prepared pigs for eating.
So the Spanish named the animals "pigs."

A book about cavies explains the "guinea" part this way:
Early English sailors often collected cavies on their
voyages to South America. When the sailors returned to
England, they sold the animals for a guinea each. (A
guinea was an early English coin.) So the English added
guinea to the name.

Hmmm . . . you never know what interesting histories
some household pets have!

What do turtles do all day ?

Y ou won't see these quiet, gentle reptiles running around exercise wheels, or "talking." To find out about a turtle's day, I trailed one, and took these slides to show you.

Click: Meet Simon the land turtle. He lives in a terrarium. A terrarium should have sand and plants like those in the natural surroundings of wild turtles.

Click: A bulb lights up the terrarium. The bulb takes the place of the sun. It keeps Simon and his surroundings warm.

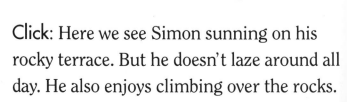

Click: Here we see Simon sunning on his rocky terrace. But he doesn't laze around all day. He also enjoys climbing over the rocks.

Click: Here is Simon crawling toward his meal. His owner has placed food on a clean little dish. "This is perfect," Simon may be thinking. His friends in the wild would, of course, have to search for their own food.

Click: Here, at the other end of the terrarium, Simon has just taken a dip in his water basin. The water in the basin just reaches the turtle's neck. At this depth, Simon easily keeps his nose above water.

Click: Sometimes Simon's owner shuts off the terrarium light, making the "sun" disappear just as it would on cloudy days if Simon lived outdoors. Here we see Simon's owner spraying the turtle. The mist reminds Simon of his natural home on rainy days.

Well, these pets have led us on quite a chase. I was a bit too brave for my own good with Tabby, but otherwise I had fun and found a lot of answers. So long for now. I hope you will join me on my next round of cases!

To Parents

Children love to ask questions. *All About Pets*, with special mouse detective McQ, will provide your child with the answers to many common questions children ask about pets. These answers will serve as a bridge into learning some important concepts. Here are a few easy and natural ways your child can express feelings and understandings about what Inspector McQ has to say. You know your child and can best judge which ideas she or he will enjoy most.

Does your child love kittens and puppies? If so, suggest making a gallery to display pictures of pets in your child's room. Give your child old magazines to find and cut out the pictures of pets. Help glue the pictures on large sheets of paper with the word *Pets* at the top. Help name each pet and add a label under the pet's picture.

Show your child how to approach and handle pets—your own if you have any, and those of people you know. Teaching your child to be careful when approaching strange animals and to be gentle with all animals will help your child learn to enjoy pets.

Matching words to pictures is a fun way to learn how to spell. Suggest making pet name and picture cards that can be matched. Your child can draw a picture of each type of pet in the book while you make a set of name cards for each pet. Then help your child match each picture with its name card and spell the pet's name.

What kinds of pets do you see most often: cats or dogs? On a trip to the store or on a family outing, count the number of dogs and cats you see. When you return home, help your child make a bar graph showing the number of each type of pet seen. Draw a bar to show the number of dogs and another bar to show the number of cats. Which bar is longer?

Help your child make a pet care check-off list, organized like a calendar, for any pets you may have. Depending on how your family shares responsibilities, the charts could have spaces for family members to initial when they have fed the fish in the morning, brushed the cat or dog at night, and so on.